ABC
See, Hear, Do

Learn to read 55 words

by Stefanie Hohl

Chou Publications

www.abcseeheardo.com

To my kids -
You are my inspiration.

Special thanks to Ryann McKinney for her hard
work and vision, and to my family and friends
who have supported me along the way.

ABC See, Hear, Do: Learn to Read 55 Words

Copyright © 2017 by Stefanie Hohl

Summary: Help your child learn letter sounds through seeing the letter, hearing the sound,
and doing an action. Blend sounds together to read three-letter words.

ISBN 978-0-9985776-0-9

How to use this book:

- Teach your child the sound each letter makes, NOT the letter name.

- Have your child make the hand motion that corresponds with each letter.

- Teach the short vowel sounds, like the "a" sound in apple, not ape.

- Work in groups of 4 letters at a time.

- Teach your child to blend sounds together to form words.

- Younger children may not be ready to blend sounds yet. For them,

  focus on learning letter sounds.

- Have fun!

This method of learning to read uses visual, auditory, and kinesthetic

learning styles to teach phonemic awareness. Your child will see the

letter, hear the sound it makes, and move his or her body, thereby

making concepts age-appropriate and easier to retain.

C...C...C

Cat

Curl your hands like
claws and scratch

Aaaaa

Ant

Throw your hands in the
air like you're scared

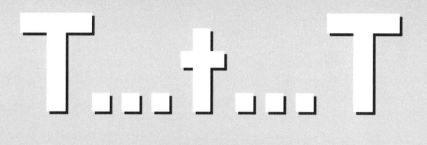

Turtle

Tap the air

Mmmm

Monkey

Rub your belly like you
ate something yummy

Hey, guess what? It's time
to read! Say the sound and
make the motion for each letter.

CAT

MAT

Now say them faster.
And faster.
Wow! Great job!

Sssss

Salamander

Make your hands
slither like a snake

Rrrrr

Raccoon

Pretend to rev
a motorcycle

Iiiii

Iguana

Wave your hands
back and forth

P....p....P

Porcupine

Open and close your hands
like they are popping

Time to read some more words!

SAT

RAT

PAT

SIP

Way to go!

B...b...B

Bear

Move your arm like you
are playing a bass drum

F...f...F

Flamingo

Flap your arms
like a flamingo

Ooooo

Octopus

Make an O with
your hands

G...g...G

Gorilla

Pretend to hold a
cup and gulp a drink

I bet you can read a few more words now.

BAT

FAT

FOG

BOG

MOP

Awesome! You've already read
20 words! Can you believe it?

L...l...L

Lion

Pretend to lick
a lollipop

J...j...J

Jaguar

Move your hands up and down
like they are jumping

Uuuuu

Umbrella Bird

Pretend to open an umbrella

H...h...H

Hippopotamus

Pretend to wipe sweat
from your forehead

Now you're really reading. Check these out:

HAT

HIP

LIP

JOG

LOG

HOG

HUT

GUT

CUT

RUT

That was 10 more words! Go you!

D...d...D

Dog

Pound one fist
on top of the other

W...w...W

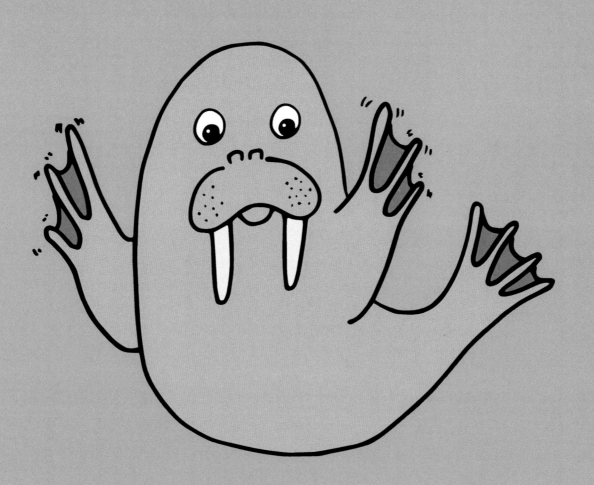

Walrus

Wiggle your fingers

Eeeee

Elephant

Put your hands around your
mouth like you're yelling

N...n...N

Narwhal

Wave one finger
back and forth

DEN

HEN

PEN

TEN

DOG

Another 10 words. Incredible!

K...k...K

Kangaroo

Pretend to turn
a key in a lock

Y...y...Y

Yak

Stretch your arms
out in a yawn

V ... v ... V

Vulture

Make a V
with your fingers

X....x....X

X-Ray Tetra Fish

Cross your arms in an X

KIN

KID

VAN

VET

YEN

Now that's impressive reading!

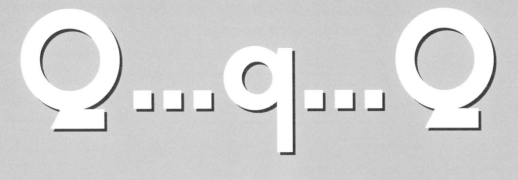

Quail

Tuck your hands in your
armpits and flap your elbows

Zzzzz

Zebra

Press your hands to your
cheek like you are sleeping

Congratulations! You just read 55 words!

Ready for a challenge? Try reading these words!

CAB	PEG	LID	HOT
JAB	BET	DIP	LOT
DAD	GET	FIT	NOT
SAD	JET	SIT	TOT
RAG	LET	FIX	BUG
WAG	NET	JOB	HUG
CAN	SET	SOB	RUG
FAN	YES	HOP	TUG
RAN	BIB	TOP	SUN
TAP	RIB	COT	CUP
FED	DID	DOT	PUP
LEG	HID	GOT	NUT

Now try reading some lowercase words!

dab	nap	rig	con
lab	fax	fin	bop
bad	tax	bit	pox
mad	led	kit	cub
pad	wed	lit	sub
bag	beg	pit	dug
gag	met	zit	jug
bam	pet	bob	lug
ham	vex	cob	mug
jam	rid	sod	bus
ram	fig	rod	but
cap	jig	mom	hut

Aa
Bb
Cc
Dd

Ee
Ff
Gg
Hh

Ii
Jj
Kk
Ll

Mm
Nn
Oo
Pp

Qq
Rr
Ss
Tt

Uu
Vv
Ww
Xx

Yy
Zz